THE NOTHING BIRD

THE NOTHING BIRD

SELECTED POEMS BY PIERRE PEUCHMAURD
TRANSLATED BY E. C. BELLI

Oberlin College Press
Oberlin, Ohio

The FIELD Translation Series, vol. 31
Oberlin College Press, 50 N. Professor Street, Oberlin, OH 44074
www.oberlin.edu/ocpress

Cover art: Robert and Shana ParkeHarrison, "Visitation" (1999)
Cover and book design: Steve Farkas

Library of Congress Cataloging-in-Publication Data

Peuchmaurd, Pierre, author.
 [Poems. Selections. English]
 The Nothing Bird : selected poems of Pierre Peuchmaurd ; translated by
E. C. Belli.
     pages cm. — (The FIELD Translation Series ; vol. 31)
   ISBN 978-0-932440-45-7 (pbk. : alk. paper) — ISBN 0-932440-45-2 (pbk. : alk.
paper)
   I. Belli, E. C., translator. II. Title.
   PQ2676.E848A2 2013
   841'.914—dc23
                                    2013032004

Contents

Translator's Introduction

Some poets are easy to situate: they self-identify as belonging to a school, they write manifestos, they are undeniably part of their *now*; their century, like an amphora, holds them, and their voices resonate within us, sometimes blending with the voices of comparable others, sometimes just bearing the slight timbre of those contemporaries.

Other poets, including Pierre Peuchmaurd, are more difficult to categorize. Peuchmaurd's poetry is not rooted in time. With a vernacular that eschews transience and with very little taste for the "politics" of poetry, Peuchmaurd held himself apart, both figuratively and literally, from most of his contemporaries. Although he published regularly, beginning in the seventies, with several prestigious editors, Peuchmaurd has remained, in comparison to Yves Bonnefoy, Michel Deguy, and others, relatively unknown.

What is the history of this poet who holds himself apart?

Pierre Peuchmaurd was born in Paris in 1948 into a household filled with books (his father, Jacques Peuchmaurd, was both an art and book critic). In 1955, editor and writer Eric Losfeld had founded a small press, which he named after his bookstore in Paris, Le Terrain Vague, and which was known for publishing controversial—sometimes "obscene"—material, with a penchant for surrealism. The bookstore was a known gathering place for surrealist thinkers and writers, and Peuchmaurd spent a lot of time there, even in his youth. At sixteen, he encountered André Breton, and from then on his affection for surrealism never waned. He became quite political, which got him expelled from high school and prompted a move to Brive, where his grandparents lived and where he was to finish his secondary education. He was very involved in the events of May '68, which he actually wrote a book about (*Plus Vivants Que Jamais*, 1968), and was invited, two years later, to appear on a

TV show on which he heavily criticized the then-current administration. This led to a brief contact with the "official" surrealist group, but his political engagement soon waned, leaving room, instead, for a life that would be entirely focused on poetry, its creation and publication, and connections with other writers.

Peuchmaurd became involved in many surrealist ventures (when there was no longer a surrealist "group" to speak of) and founded the Éditions Maintenant, the Éditions Toril, the literary journal *Le Cerceau*, and, in 1990, the Éditions Myrddin, which he directed until 2008. He was also a regular contributor to *Les Cahiers de l'Umbo*, *Le Bathyscaphe*, and many other journals. He died in 2009 in Brive from lung cancer, leaving two sons, Guillaume and Antoine, and his companion Anne-Marie Beeckman, as well as many friends and collaborators.*

Peuchmaurd credited two volumes as being at the origin of his poetic endeavors: *Nadja*, by André Breton, and *Les Filles du Feu*, by Gérard de Nerval. Somewhat later, he discovered Lewis Carroll and Kafka. Everything that followed was a result of those encounters (Hobbé). Peuchmaurd wrote his first poem at thirteen, sitting in his bed one morning, and called the experience a "true physical shock comparable only to that of falling in love." The world, for him, became "boundless" (Morin).

Perhaps because of this, Peuchmaurd never traveled much. "For me everything is a journey," he wrote. "A real journey, in my mind, is when a place starts talking to you *immediately*, demands to be *told* on the spot." He did spend a lot of time walking, though, and, as he rarely had anything to write with, his walks came to affect his creative process: "I must memorize what was said, and it is only once I am home that I can write it down." The poems apparently changed very little between their initial iteration, in Peuchmaurd's mind, and the start of their life on paper (Hobbé). As a reader, Peuchmaurd also liked seeing a poem in a single glance. Anne-Marie Beeckman explains that

---

* Biographical material is drawn from Laurent Albarracin.

some of the longer poems (notably from *Perfect Hurts*) were written fast, almost without lifting his pen. This process may also lie at the root of two issues readers will encounter in Peuchmaurd's work: seemingly haphazard punctuation and capitalization. Those were and are, in French, sometimes distracting, yet after much reflection I have left them in English. While the temptation to correct them is strong, I operated under the assumption that the lines Peuchmaurd capitalized were meant to draw more attention to themselves and that the errant or stray commas marked some pause—and that both must be respected.

Peuchmaurd claims that poetry concerns itself mostly with the *world*—though his description of what that means accounts for the surrealism in his work as well: "there is another world, you know. It is here and is just asking to appear" (Blanchet). Laurent Albarracin speaks of what rests at the heart of Peuchmaurd's work: "Those poems don't criticize anything, they make us see, for they are the echoes of commotions in the senses of the author.... At the heart of this poetry, there is but the living shock of the seen thing. Its violence, its emotional ramifications, nothing else" (Albarracin 2007). The world, its matter, creates a shock in the author's senses, and his interior tongue is triggered. Peuchmaurd claims that language is a consequence; it is never origin, despite all of his music, despite all of his strangely mangled idioms.

For Peuchmaurd, the greatest shock of all, the deepest impression life can impart and leave echoing within us, is desire. Eros is therefore a constant in these poems. "You are right," he says in an interview, "my poetry is mostly love poetry.... I haven't traveled much, and thought very little of matters outside of love. But my poems are also full of colors, creatures. And they are full of death. It is a poetry of fear" (Colaux). Love and death, Eros and Thanatos, are his two great, intertwined subjects.

And about the "creatures" he refers to—his wolves, his cats, his foxes, and of course, his birds? They have no symbolic role, he claims, and his poems are not to be considered a bestiary. They are nothing but themselves, echoes of the world, digested by the poet, handed back to us. "They just are," he claims (Blanchet).

Jean Follain comes to mind when we encounter Peuchmaurd's depiction of each item, plucked from the world and assigned a tone. There is a certain objectivity, a certain bewilderment in the face of the things that fill our little universes: our homes, our gardens, our countrysides. And there is a touch of Max Jacob in the fear that fills the lines—the awareness of death looming, peering from the corner, a guest, in every room. We find too a touch of René Char: the sense that we are handed something of the world, but something that has been turned inside out—that we are dealing perhaps with a negative of the world, or the world captured and returned to us warped: everything is there, it is just a degree or so off—Peuchmaurd actually speaks of a "negative of snow" in "After You." Though he never cites them as having directly inspired him, those, I believe, are Peuchmaurd's literary forebears—writers whose work, similarly, seems to have been unaffected by time.

This is not meant to be a definitive translation. Instead, I invite readers to think of this volume as my personal foray into a poet whose work utterly charmed me when I first encountered "A Treatise on Wolves" some three or four years ago, and found it peering back at me with all of its feral and tender madness.

The process of translation was, on the most obvious level, relatively easy for me, as I was fortunate enough to grow up bilingual. But this very familiarity with both languages sometimes made the process more difficult. Indeed, while Peuchmaurd's French was no doubt affected by his time in Paris, Brive, and Cazillac, mine was affected by growing up outside of Geneva. And while my English was affected by the fact that I learned it from my British mother, Peuchmaurd's texts had to exist in American English and all of its various quirks.

Another great difficulty for the translator may lie in guessing what associations Peuchmaurd might have made in his mind—given his allegiance to surrealism and the "directed automatism" he sometimes used (Hobbé)—without performing what he referred to as a "paranoid" interpretation of his work: infusing his lines with a purpose or meaning they do not have.

Titles, of course, bore a certain pressure. "Frictions" was, in the French, "Râpes," which literally translated can be some kind of grater, rasp, or grinder. I asked Anne-Marie Beeckman what she believed Peuchmaurd meant, and she encouraged me to let it summon anything that scrapes or that is rough like sandpaper. Those small prose poems are "scrapy"—they leave the reader unsettled, raw. "Frictions" seemed to adequately capture this, while at the same time alluding to the idea of "fiction" and the narrative nature of the poems.

"The Tiger and the Signifier" was, in its original, "Le Tigre et la chose signifiée." It was clear from the era during which Peuchmaurd was writing that issues of signifiers and signifieds were present, and Anne-Marie confirmed my suspicion that the title might allude to structuralist woes (Peuchmaurd abhorred rhetoric and theory). "Signifier" won for its music when paired with "The Tiger," since sound is oftentimes at the heart of Peuchmaurd's endeavors.

In the poems themselves, I encountered a number of difficulties. For instance, in "Written for the Occasion," the passage "des combats de basse lice" posed some problems. At first glance, "combats" literally translates to "combats" or "fights," and "lice" signifies the wooden barriers used to contain a tourney or a joust (an upper border contains the fight and a lower border creates a pen of sorts for the aides). "Basse" would seem to refer to this "low" border, but it is an unusual turn of phrase. "Basse-lice" exists too—and more commonly—as an expression that can be translated to "low-warp" (as in a low-warp tapestry). I believe the ambiguity and Peuchmaurd's desire to mix fighting and weaving in our minds to be intentional, and so this landed me with "low-warp combats," which is as strange in English as it is in French.

Another example of a difficult choice concerns a tricky passage from "The Wind in April 2007": "un merle par an milan dans la perle," which literally translates to "one blackbird a year kite in the pearl/dew" (one variety of the bird known as the kite is the pearl kite). To complicate things further, "milan" is a homonym of "mille ans," which signifies "a thousand years." The ear is tempted to hear, in French, "one blackbird a year a thousand years in the pearl." Sadly all of these complexities could not be reproduced, and I settled for "one blackbird a year a kite in the dewdrop," to preserve, at least, the rich imagery.

I also made a few choices for the sake of flow. In "Boulevard des Invalides," I replaced what should have been "map of the sky" with "face of the sky." Though a slight departure, "face" conveyed the sense of something lined, something that could be mapped, while at the same time preserving soundplay ("you don't pin lace / onto the face of the sky"). In "The Night," a literal translation would read: "No one the lamp no one the temples." While a temple is both a body part and an architectural event in English, it is a body part only in French. To clear this up and to allow the line to sing, I added "on either side of the face."

Of Peuchmaurd, I first knew but wolves and his end, which has sadly robbed us of more work. Linh Dinh says, "Translation, like jazz, is a form of revenge." My hope is that *The Nothing Bird* can be revenge for an end, a stay against the world—its time-bound spirit—and the beginning of many conversations on the great Pierre Peuchmaurd.

E. C. Belli

Works Cited

Albarracin, Laurent. Contribution to the French poetry blog *Poezibao*. 30 April 2009. http://poezibao.typepad.com/poezibao/2009/04/pierre-peuchmaurd.html.

———. *Pierre Peuchmaurd Témoin Élégant*. Montréal: L'Oie de Cravan. 2007.

———. *Présence de la Poésie: Pierre Peuchmaurd*. Montreuil-sur-Brèche: Éditions des Vanneaux. 2011.

Beeckman, Anne-Marie. Personal letter to the translator (December 2012).

Bériou, Jean-Yves. "La criminelle beauté du monde: la poésie de Pierre Peuchmaurd." Translated into Spanish by Miguel Casado for *Animal Sospechoso* (Barcelona) 5-7 (2009).

Blanchet, Marc. Interview with Pierre Peuchmaurd. *Le Matricule des Anges* 54 (2004).

Colaux, Denys-Louis. Interview with Pierre Peuchmaurd. *Styloscopie*, Le Grand-Hors-Jeu, 67 (1992).

Hobbé, Olivier. Interview with Pierre Peuchmaurd. *Quimper est poésie* 29 (2000).

Morin, Georges-Henri. "Pierre Peuchmaurd, la poésie et 'le peu de réalité.'" *Contre'Temps* 12 (2012).

from *The Nothing Bird* (1984)

A Treatise on Wolves

for Antoine

At night the wolves are blue, a little phosphorescent.

There are wolves, you know, who peer out of windows and see the distance. Wolves who weep for their silent prey.

There are wolves who spread rumors pink and yellow, wolves who lick the necks of lace makers, furtive wolves, seasonal wolves. Jealous wolves in foreign cities.

There is winter blooming.

There are scholarly wolves who sleep in books, hermit and synthetic wolves. Absent, very, very absent wolves, wolves with no heart, the best wolves.

There are clay and wallpaper wolves. Arabian wolves with green turbans, occasional wolves and unconditional wolves. Certain wolves are trouble-free and the wind blows through them.

There are sun wolves. The shade wishes them well as they watch the sea. There are wolves like that.

Wolves don't always dream, but sometimes they will.

Spring wolves, discount wolves. Intangible wolves who wear stockings and red lipstick on their chops. Chilly wolves, with feelings. Golden wolves.

There are oblique wolves who leave by day, who leave by night, and hopeless wolves with a look wolves should have.

There are furious wolves, wolves who think about wolves and wolves who think about whales. Under the wolves' pillows, there are crime novels.

There is the hunger of wolves.

Some wolves, you know, have no memory, no pack. Often, they are young wolves in search of a face on which to lay their velvet coats.

And then, there are she-wolves.

from Short Frictions

After they had both melted into the pink sheets of sundown, dark machines began to produce pleasure. They would be taken away the next day; they knew it. The night was short, the morning haggard.

A hundred thousand years later, molded in the pink sheets of sundown, dark machines produce pleasure, desire, pleasure, desire, pleasure, pleasure.

CHILDHOOD

Green smoke and clay sheep, it's like a moor at the end of the earth, the ghosts there, the rapiers, the moon-wells even in April. It's all Irish with wind.

Now starts running. Now is twelve years old. Like a forest at the end of the seas.

Gigantic and rotten: the roses.

SUNDAY

Shadows, like a whim of light. Shadows too that part us.

Listless sun on the gravel, on the porch, on the floorboards, in the mirror, and in your bed. And in your bed.

Floors. Skirts rumpling. The rules of the game.

In the attic, the hanged are talking about their childhood.

THE JOURNEY

I knew where I was going. In the sky, there are blue stones and in my head little rules. *I don't take shadows from anyone*—that and other such things you'd tell yourself on a journey.

The train was empty, or almost. Entire days went by without me. Men, women deserted their love. The summer was there.

In every town I crossed, mirrors fogged up.

Art Objects, Six Frights

This is where they come to shoot. Why here, and to shoot what?
It's always in the evening, when you can barely see a thing. They
aim obscurely at night, the hunters. Are they even hunters?
When the wind picks up, it's as though the echo of this very old
war has returned to haunt the edge of the woods. It tells us that
there's no safe refuge, and no forgetting either. You never see the
hunters. No one skims the woods at this hour, or at other hours
for that matter—in the morning, perhaps. But not me. In the
morning, I sleep.

THE COURTYARD

The courtyard has four trees, tires, and a bear. The trees are chestnut trees. There is another tree, a fifth one, with pink flowers sometimes. The tires are just tires. They were for the children, I think. To play on. The bear, ever since he ate his keeper, cannot remember what he is doing there.

THE STABLE

The stable is bare, but well insulated. The presence of that hanged man, in the back, near the feeders, solicits no particular remarks: the rope is his. What is deplorable however is this sudden proliferation of flies, those blue ones, those green ones. Bloated, how often they fall into the milk. The tepid foam engulfs them and then, yes, of course, he draws attention to himself. But what can we do? The flies are his too.

THE WALL

The grey and yellow wall, the only one in the entire country,
performs somewhat random and equivocal acts of kindness.
For ivy, for a thorn, it'll do what it has to. It knows how to
make itself welcoming to toads, to dogs. It doesn't want any
trouble with its shadow. But when a man presses a woman up
against it, the wall closes in on them. Every time.

THE OFFICE

At the end of the hall, a red door with scratch marks. It's the divine office, the dead bird in its feathers and its reflection too in the shade. There is a dead bird reciting the divine office, an enormous bird. He's been put there by mistake. Dead birds are for girls.

THE ROOM

Nowadays, the room doesn't scare many people. It's easy to believe that it was once constantly occupied. And not only by lovers: by the lovers of lovers and by their obscure accomplices. Reluctantly, they admit to you that many a silence was heard coming from the room. But those are rumors, they add. There was a well in the room. That's where it all came from. And will come again, so they say.

from *The Fiddler Crab* (1991)

from Life in the Countryside

for Anne Marbrun

SUNDAY

A chainsaw maims the air. It's Sunday, and there's that perfect Sunday dread. You dream of long dawns, of sailboats in a harbor, of long shots of rum inside stained glass windows. You dream of a woman in her furs with blue highlights. You close your eyes a little and it's already evening. It's the silence that wakes you. The chainsaw has grown quiet. The air is gone. In its place nothing but a heavy black tapestry that the fire licks softly.

THE CATS

At night under the orange fig tree, the cats like pretending they're strange. Don't fall for it. There is nothing more natural than those shapes, those adornments, those wounds. You must understand: they are our little princes. At dawn, they join us in our undone sheets. They join our wives mostly. That, too, you must understand.

THE OLD WASHHOUSE

The strawberries of the old washhouse, the clockwork storm in your doll head, those fanatic, blue, and really tiny dwarves, the hollow path, the wool, those five other spells, the strawberries—I don't think I'm forgetting anything. Sometimes, you'd come apart. Your legs would start quivering. And then your nervous breathing got so frantic I thought it might stop for good. And you'd moan; you moaned in a terrible silence (I don't think I'm forgetting anything). I'd touch you. Only then, I'd touch you.

At night, the animals pass through us. We are not the ones they seek, they want. And yet, they leave a trace. Waking, we gaze at each other, surprised, tired. There lingers in the bed a sharp smell of the wild that is neither languor nor pleasure. It's from the animals.

CLOSURE

In the end, it was raining. It was a day for apples, for walnuts, for medium heat. You were bored. Long red slugs were part of it.

from *In Settlement for All Dreams* (1998)

April's Wolf

October's wolf
his white coat on the leaves
his salted tongue on the water
his eyes in the hallway
Wolf that the wind crosses
that a single dream stuns

April's wolf, antique apple

Clack go the crows
in the knife air
the snow pulls
its blue houses away,
they go blooming
rotting into the sea

Great weary anemones
light up the calves' foreheads

There's some dead cloud left
green flowers on our heads
and the foxes of despair,
their white spoons in their
white mouths
There's more than a season left
to wheel the shade of the old coaches around
to beat the bone against the lace

They don't live too long
those countryside cats
or the wolves in our lives
The Egyptian, she is bare
the sailor black
Neither the keys nor the axes
open the doors anymore

⌀

Chained dazzled
the two girls with the mirror
all ankles and ivory
are breaking their bones
kissing their lips
Are planting stakes
in the snow

⌀

Patios of cold,
of ink jets in the upheaval,
patios prey
to the russet star

What is this thing you are holding—
a promise or a banister?

⌀

That yellow place beside your shadow
the slope of parties and hillsides
that we walked along evening after evening—

the yellow place where the rain came
to set my age upon your shoulders,
a dog sniffs the place a dog sleeps there
wrapped in its great feathers

Ø

The horse has placed
his skull upon the gate
Where it whinnies all night
It whinnies the ennui
of the great flowers that carve it
The great flowers carve
the dawn inside the horse's chest

Ø

Those empty wheels
the air of the rooms
in summer at three p.m.
descending into the valley
without a dog without a weapon

Ø

White gillyflowers the bull's bath
the rain barking with its lunar tongues
Black horizon white gillyflowers
the victors are still
those who sleep soundest at night

Ø

The Guarantors of Sleep
the Keepers of the Peace in outdoor clothing
the Heads of the Exhaustion Department
the Administration of the Walls
Small homes small concerts

∅

Under the tree, revenge
Under the tree, at the foot of the sky
With whips of flesh
against the soft soil of the heart
With twenty years of thorns
to punish exhaustion,
the pale roses of the summons

∅

Of course, it's easy to forget
like that winter the lion rejects
Of course, the flesh is strong
birds throw their meat into the sky
Of course, you weren't
that angelic light, that arm of the Loire River

from *The Loris-Atlantique* (1999)

Twelve Torments

I was something of a wild carrot, quite far from hope. The wind, which is the feeling of being alive, rarely came down to see me. Slugs gnawed at my foot. I even saw the war go by. I don't know who or what put an end to it all.

I was waterfall. A thousand girls ran off of my boulders. The Enchanter liked it and I liked the Enchanter. And now, a stalactite where the night freezes her teeth, where the birds are silent.

I was an ancient bear, uncouth, wrongly hurt. Three arrows in the flank don't add up to one death, a red stream doesn't make a sound. The shadow of the moons passes over the wound.

I was a hay-pack, a dog-stack, a crowd of hips. Poor, with grand dresses, I was the faraway mule that gets slaughtered in autumn.

I was a scrap of Normandy or the night tightening over Granville. I was a flatfish. The sky often changed. I watched the white shades of asphyxiation move, shimmer, and darken.

I had been a sheep or a crow or nothing at all. I was my skull tossed far from my carcass. When I spell the word heath, I spell it with your heart.

I was the ripped wing of a condor or of a fly. In the shade in which I bled, the dust was white; I was thirsty for the body of a redhead, for a shoulder upon which to sing.

I was the devil's sandal, and no earth below, not a blade of grass, not a girl, not a fire in which to lie. I was the devil's only sandal and nothing much held me.

I was the ninth brandy after the burial, the one that kicks you into the ditch. I was waiting for the tears to come, or the scream, or the laughter; I was waiting for the horse to go by. And the earth drank me.

I was a wet towel that the sea soaked and the evening wrung out. And I was the pale towel where young skies and visitations slept. And that man with a blue forehead was cutting the grass of the wind.

I was the toad's uncle—a very old thing indeed, I must say. I was a sky of snow, I was a watching eye that does not understand what it is seeing. I was that yellow light and nothing turned me off.

I am the head of the mona monkey, its open throat (glass case, larynx, and subservience included) on the ground floor of the museum. I am smiling at you from the depths of death and torment.

from *The Twisted Eye* (2003)

The Twisted Eye

The grass turns pale just remembering their names. Those who already came: Death, Ennui, Love, and Tides, we know them well. Death, on its blue horse. Ennui, turning the pages, Love tearing them apart. Tides: their tigers, their limps. Must we really meet them again, each spring of each life, and feel them inside of every woman?

𝄞

We told earth: she would be traveled by powerful white herds. That young winds would push young horses toward young precipices. That the fire would drink snow, that the fire would give carcasses wings, push soft worms into stomachs, and tie butterflies to mouths that wouldn't say no. The earth was warned, she didn't say no.

𝄞

Across the marble floors of the courtyards, long trails of blood. The water runs red in the fountains and the curtains are black. We don't know where this blood is coming from.

𝄞

Cream: part cry, part ream. They spread cream all over the crime scene and called it speech, and called it gardens, stormy nights, mad love. They fastened sails onto nightfall, windows onto daybreak, white gloves onto the sleepers' hands and called it thought. They took their time, took more time. Now they wait.

𝄞

The girl laughed, teeth wide apart, like a drop of grenades over pale water. In the blue sky, a split carcass, the deer rots.

∅

At the edge of the woods, a white creature shimmers in the shade, in the air. We remember. We aren't sure what, but we remember: the light was green and golden. We are given girlfriends, wives, yet we want sisters, creatures white, naked, fierce, and mortal. But not fierce for our sake. And not mortal for our sake either.

∅

Dusk. A bat crosses the moon. Flies back and forth between the eye of the observer and the yellow disc. The observer is a badger, a barn owl, a roebuck covered in blood—something that can't remember, something that can forget us.

∅

When the mist rises from the river, the big crow bangs at the window, demanding a loaf of *pain de neige*, and repeats the question. There are no loaves left, the crow's question is pointless. We posed it to the wind, the poplars, the pebbles, and to love's scattered members too. The scattered members of love do not answer such questions.

∅

Hanging from the cows' necks, the dead eyes of the first monkeys jingle, deep within the mountain. Other baroquisms: the feathers the donkey left to the white bushes, used to cover young leprous women, the marbles lost by the torrents, the gold rats, the purple she-dwarves, the double skeletons, the final ends. Hips and projects.

∅

It was a shoulder, but isn't anything anymore: the flesh of the maze cracks under the weight of the cannibalistic ox's molar. Herbage, there's no cure, he needs that red flower, that pink mucus, the quivering of these thighs from the warmth of that snout. He needs the black eye that has turned in its orbit to turn blind to itself. Of the girl without horns, there is but one bone left.

∅

Large chests full of weapons and winter tossed onto carpets of tides: it's the war. Watch the thickets turn blue. Watch, in the dawn, the metal laughing, the hanged man we light up every night and the girls wringing their braids. Ships full of red-haired bodies. Heavy ships of rats toppling in an empty pair of eyes.

∅

Rugged tables of wine and of the sea's many tongues—the shadow of the lighthouse is its light, its solar peace, and the big white horse, the horrendous white horse, turns his white eye only once toward the drinkers. They all rise in silence, and after they pass the lighthouse, oblivion wipes the slate clean, for all, and arranges the horrendous white horse in its cardboard box.

September Alone

A quarter of a cloud, a third of a weasel—the summer is breaking its hand-painted plates. Fragments of the absolute, they shimmer deep inside the courtyards. It is dead here. Violence, boredom, disgust, melancholy.

Red-pawed prince, your head rests on the blaze's cold knees, your head rests in agony.

∅

The blue wood of the carts with the blue heads they carry toward their final blue sky. The russet feel of the earth that rises in September. The russet rivers that rise.

The creature wraps around the water the way weariness wraps the evening. The night will be long. In tree time. Time for whipping and for silence.

∅

The dogs of the queens are barking: see, it's autumn come running with its tongues hanging out, painting these strokes of sorrow in the fading grass. It's that old impatience, the freshly flesh.

The carved wooden wolf in his den, the calf's pallet of water, the naked god (it's a worm), the day that crawls on the ponds.

∅

The little animals of the sun try to milk the big animals of sleep. The big animals of sleep try harder to milk the night's dark cries. The night talks in her sleep of the wolf that takes her.

He is tiny.* His coat fits in my hands, his fur on your breasts. We picked him apart as best we could. You had a smile and I had it too. We never asked his name.

∅

Your limbs. The pale thrill of the curve of your spine as it breaks my fall, and this bramble where I build you. The wound that adorns your mouth. Let that soft deposit of blood be when September turns its horses toward the sea.

Snow of flesh, a seated dream, the world grinding up its little wooden bells. Someone arrives, and it is a horse. Someone is living in the tent of the gods. Turquoise stones and flies are beating against the washhouse.

∅

The blue hell, tomorrow's crazed hawk hurled after yesterday's. When it was always time to hunt, it was time to do homework, and you dressed those girls of reason in feathers. September sticks a heart through the sharp feather in its cap.

If you touch the snow's stomach, death will smile at you; if you don't, she will laugh. This instant is still so far ahead and yet it's already behind us, and it's in each passing moment. If you touch her breasts, death will come after you.

∅

First wet scent. First delights without you, and the acrid wine of the wind. First sip of time.

---

* The wolf that takes her.

A day without wells is a lost truth. September without a mirror, September without a sword, an autumn of paper. The blood of the dogs smolders on the hillside, the night spreads from woman to woman.

℘

The stag's feathers in the storefront window. The battle and the sand, the scales of thirst, the hard scales of your silence. Time grows timorous; we are going to die, we look so alike.

The white sink, the grey bowl, the blackout. The white face of the cow nailed to the pillowcase. The black bone of the gypsy bangs at the North's windowpane.

from *The Tiger and the Signifier* (2006)

The Lovers

The first time they're naked, they kneel. They don't look at each other, they see each other. Whether they'll touch isn't clear. They've been inside each other forever. And yet, he touches her. Eyelash to nipple, his hand traces the impossibly obvious. Each is the other's flesh already, its abandon, its splendor. The coming light of day comes across their lips.

Desire, pleasure are dark words. They tumble in their minds like rain in the springtime. Their heads separate only when it's time to speak again.

A single sigh. A root for lightning.

They open the streets: nobody sees. They are so transparent, the light doesn't know how to touch them.

Such lightness of being. Such darkness within.

Suddenly, between them, that fearsome end. The crack.

Blood on feathers. They laugh out of the same mouth, grow silent in synchrony.

There's no bottom to the depths of their bed.

She has lighter eyes, he has her eyes. They've loved each other since exchanging names.

Once in the room, they'll never come out. Flattering reality is no longer their concern.

Blood on feathers, they're the peafowl, the fan, the whole thing.

On the whole.

They see their casket, their crypt, the cart that holds their ashes. Such a huge fire.

The Images

for Anne-Marie Beeckman

It's hard milk, sweet marble, it's your body below the moon, it's Sunday night, the door open, the sea inside.

⌀

It runs through stones, golden, it turns blue: it could be pink as fanned fingers. It skitters and sings.

⌀

It's round, and it's divided for the length of your reign. As you rush your night forward, you puncture the day. A drum under the thunder, a sacrificial goat, tall trees like red organ pipes.

⌀

To see better, you close your eyes. Under your hands, astonishing, the sky goes by. A confusion of wings undoes the hedge.

⌀

Night conceals tips of sunlight, flowers and flint, green and white birds, rapiers, childhood. Night, and your face.

⌀

Wood burns, knees bend, tongues lick clouds to a luster.

The Foam of Lions

*It's raining, we count the hearts of the palm tree. Elsewhere, a wall
burns against a white sky, blue lions sigh after blue prey. But lions, you
say, don't sigh. I watch their prey, I sigh. The desert's door has closed
behind us.*

⌀

Their tails whip the sand. In the air, a mane floats within reach
of your lips. Three yellow-eyed lionesses have arched their
spines well, but against the wind brushing the earth, not the
large absent limb you bite in your dream. A white rafter holds
the night.

⌀

Obscure lions in hallways, but where do they go? Weightless,
the lions under the waterfalls, pounded white, their bones, their
flesh tossed to the world, the foam of lions. They're startled by
the persistence of their thirst, by the gazelle that laughs in her
sleep, by the girl from the sky with lead fangs.

⌀

Copper lions, bracelets of bone, and those strange *nabules*
tintinabulating at nightfall. The black hunter strings his harp
into the morning. The sky is high, the bird from the water flies
like a lion. Cargos of roses, trains of dust, the harp is stringed
and the lion no longer has a shadow. Trains of dust, copper
blood.

⌀

At noon, the lions are a speck of sand. At noon, the lions are smoke rings, rafts of light, hedges of lace, mirages of salt and emerald. At noon, the lions have closed their eyes to the expectation of night that will see them standing tall and tamed and licking your stomach—the night of blood curdled on your rumps, on your ruins.

℘

But in the dream of the lionesses, one or one thousand is all the same. Everything roars, everything falls silent; the dawn does not lift a breath. What was that zebra called again?

Before the End

It could be a childhood memory. You'd buy it for almost
nothing, end it in a blind alley.

It could be dusk, there'd be a fountain fire.

It could be ten p.m., we'd be soaked to the bone, to the white
flowers of our bones.

It could still be the daytime. It could be more than just daytime.

It could be in the suburbs, but seem like the edge of the forest.
The air could be green, the words yellow.

It could be a horse, lost right there where it's been found, a
horse in its mist, licking your stockings,

a telephone next to a manncquin.

It could still be the daytime.

Right before the end.

It could be more than just daytime.

It could be a faraway cry gone off its course, a man fishing for gold at low tide.

It could be the road that goes there, the one that doesn't.

It could be the earth in the shade, the ash of waterfalls.

And just before the end,

it could still be the daytime.

At least, we'd see to it.

Glimmers

The glimmers of our world: the river crow spreading its wide blue wings in the drowning shade.

ɸ

On a yellow stone, a white mane—a glimmer of wind.

ɸ

Glimmers of fire in the mirror: the auburn one returning, all body and tides.

ɸ

Glimmers of fear: like a necklace dangling between your breasts, snapped by the night's shrill cry.

ɸ

Glimmers of dawn, a barbed dance. Glimmer of the trees—we must leave.

ɸ

This is no white creature, this is a hole in the sky.

ɸ

The glimmers of the wolf, a glowing she-wolf—a dogwood barks in their joint song.

ɸ

Rock or heather. The glimmers of the roosters. Desire ruffles the crests, the countryside and its moons.

⌀

The glimmers of vines: wrestlers bound by their lion spirit, their spears and their indigo blue.

⌀

It's a king, it's a chair, it's a lighthouse standing in the clay.

⌀

The glimmers of lakes, of iron, of girls. Glimmers of fog and of bare land.

⌀

The glimmer of feathers, of little dresses, of remorse. Glimmers of blood in the garden.

⌀

It's a shoulder.

⌀

The glimmers of arrows. The glimmers of otters inside their prey.

⌀

And rust in the hands left open. The glimmers of the wounds along the knife.

⌀

The sand glimmers like nothing, like nothing glimmers, like sky and lead on the patio. The sand runs, it does not glimmer.

from *Perfect Hurts and Other Achievements*
(2007)

Boulevard des Invalides

I saw it this morning:
twenty-five years, my love,
twenty-five years have gone by.

You don't ever take them out anymore
your painted wood scarecrow
your clear day companion
You don't take out your horses
your madmen and whales
you don't arrange your seagulls
in the seagull drawer
you don't have animals anymore
or much hope
you don't light the fire
more than once or twice a summer
you don't sleep in the snow
you don't hunt the cherries
with your great glad airs
and it's rare, it's quite rare
for you to remember me
our fear, laughter
and six p.m. trains
You don't rumple the laundry
of the forests
you don't pin lace
onto the face of the sky
you don't open your wings
or just open them a little
and you never fly off
much farther than the end
of last winter
when we followed the stream

embroidered with
balustrades that had white
or green highlights
which lasted until night
You don't last until night

Today
more easily than in the past
when I used to hold the key to it
I wander in your emptiness
I say more easily
because it's been empty of you since
it's been empty of me
I don't even see that
spear planted in the morning anymore
Boulevard des Invalides
I don't picture your voice
Yet I know—
the down of your body
still burns inside the earth
the wind along your shoulders
still makes that husky chant
but you no longer have shoulders
you don't even have wings
and the lioness tosses
in her bed of dead wood
and every Sunday writes
to Sundays that were
and the envelopes are empty inside
like those shelves under the sea
with their empty boats
and empty fishes
you don't bring in your wolves
you don't take off your gloves
to stroke the rain

you don't have
naked fingers left under all of those rings
that naked mouth amid the haze
those knees, those pigeons
those clouds along your breasts
you don't come back in at night
with your big cold beasts
and that smell of the city
far away the black alleys
and I don't know your neck anymore
or your nape that moved slowly
in the heavy air for me alone
You won't even bring
the coal bucket into
your purple house anymore
with your fifteen fur coats on,
or those little nuggets of water
Now even your tongue is dead
though I still speak it

A Few of the Words I Was Mysteriously Allowed Until Now

for Antoine

The word promises left first
no one made them anymore
The word sky followed
the word sky always follows
The words forest river morning
the word fox the great word wolf
already ghostly apparitions
The word house seemed fragile
the word mist dissipated
The word washbasin drowned
in its own clamor taking cats with it
The words star cardboard whale
Shade kept its weight
though more inept more solemn
The word desire wore itself out
spilling everywhere
the word tide receded
The words lightning thorn and hawk
the word small the word bird
those words ah! those words
Grass dried on foot
the word mirror had already shattered
even the word breasts no longer caused a surge
The word go stayed
longed to go
stayed
The word seasons ran idle
The word regret the word futile
Everything let me go
Everything,
to a certain extent

It Will Come in My Left Lung

It will come in my left lung
At first it will feel warmer
and then will spread throughout,
I'll say that I'm all right.
It will be like snow—
I hate the snow—
like a sip of coffee
when you don't have the heart for it.
And then I will deny it.
How substantial my denial?
And how long will things last?
For the life of a rose, not even a rose?
That is how you must count
when there is that spume,
all that pretty crimson blood
rising like a tide onto the lips.
You count in birds,
in hoops around the field,
in rivers inside the summer
and in forevers.
You count on the fingers of women
and the hair of creatures
that never falls into the sink,
you count on the good weather
that opens your throat.
The women,
since you are about to die,
the women open their dresses—
you count on that.
And since you're about to go,
they leave you their addresses
and the night takes them away
and you go into the woods
where the hospital is.

The Watchman

The river was high
and the earth drank from it
and great dead birds
flew above it all
(there was at least one)
and the watchman sang
his watchman song
of not waiting for fall
of not waiting for winter
of waiting for spring
and for the first red stain
on the flanks of the girls from the sky
and the watchman watched
his black and white song
and that very first horse
on that very first star
and the river knitted
a shroud for the storms
heard from afar
aging in a glass of water
away from the eyes of the watchman
who was looking at his hands
who was looking at nothing
who was digging in the sand
digging tunnels in the sky
who was waiting for fall
who was waiting for winter
and for the mare of the night
and for ennui to speak with him
the song of the watchmen

Furniture

O the dappled skies of love
but beware in the stairway
there are dogs wolves pipe organs
and a giraffe on each landing
Beware the chairs
chairs are shooting stars
and beware the box tree in the yard,
the deaf cry of the box tree
and beware the bed where
the deaf cry of the box tree goes to hide
Beware the elephants, they're all trunk
and beware the schoolgirls
who hide things in drawers
Beware of attics
of their heat
of the straw covering the fire of scorned girls,
mattresses mannequins and prophecies
beware of attics
Beware of mirrors beware the pink waters
of living rooms and lakes that hide slaughterhouses
beware of bathtubs
of plastic whales and iguanodons
beware remorse deep inside the sink
beware the candied orange swimming pools
overlain with she-foxes
Beware the kitchens where pharaohs go
beware of the garden shed and the strawberry furnace
of closets, wardrobes, and beware the wash
Specifically, beware the yellow wash of summer
in the dark night of wardrobes
Beware of monsoons and monkeys
beware the curtains

the barnyards in rain
fat limp turkeys that carry disaster
Beware especially of rabbit hutches,
rabbit hutches and pedestal tables
Beware of paintings, especially still lifes
especially portraits especially landscapes,
beware bison that carry limp turkeys
that carry disaster
Beware of lamps of silhouettes of hallways,
boys and scarabs speak there in cursed tongues
and sometimes sacred tongues
that make all things blush
Beware things that blush
and cassis at the bottom of glasses
Beware libraries, stolen books without jackets
walking into cellars
O beware of cellars,
of leprosy and wine
of turbulent cellar winds
Beware of greenhouses, eagles grow there flowers fly
beware of livestock
heifers were spotted in the father's room
Beware of dressers
and the heads of chickadees
and beware the well in the grass
Beware of roof tiles
at night the tiles fly off in search of day
Beware of sponges pitchers of milk and replicas
beware of the VCR and avoid using the telephone
beware of armor and taxidermied creatures
and taxidermied women
and beware of drafts
Beware of barns and the fatalist men hanging there
be very afraid of grooms, and therefore beware of stables
beware pianos and their prehensile tails

beware of couches of lions of turtles
and of the Galapagos,
it's another climate
Beware especially of planispheres, of compact powder
and of novels left open on that page with the chaise lounge,
beware that shawl (it's no coincidence)
Beware the elevator,
there usually isn't one
Beware knives forks and desserts
don't get a second dessert
beware the eyeglasses forgotten on the dune
and if there is no dune beware the sea
Beware of fear
beware the parking lot, that's where they'll be waiting for you
beware of morning,
of evening of ink and springtime
And beware the dappled skies

After You

Preceded by birds by moons by scorpions
preceded by silence, by the great sound of silence
preceded by dawns by shop windows by waterfalls
preceded by your breasts and the ramp to the casino
by the waterfalls of your back against my nape
by my nape against your falls
by my nape for all of those blows
preceded by a storm and a marital status
preceded
(I don't have the patience I'd)
preceded
(need to not
love y-
ou, to speak of the)
preceded
(light on the hillsides
I don't have)
preceded
(that)
preceded by skinned
sheep and by pigs
preceded by slaughterhouses
and by windmills with their ruins,
by carcasses and dreadful fears
preceded by softness, by favors, preceded
by your hands
preceded by black flowers and by little balls of spring
by the crimson hunt, preceded by the crimson hunt
preceded by a shortly-before-the-end-of-days sunshine
and by its negative of snow
preceded by the naked earth and entwined felines
preceded by rumors and the snake's cry

by a *vin de voile* and by a star
(not enough eyes, I don't have enough eyes)
and preceded by despair
and preceded (my heart all Egypt) by a desert and by a doubt,
by ribbons and chains
preceded by the jewels of necessity
preceded by giantesses more flexible than death
as scared as your own fear
preceded by ancient laughter,
by a little girl on the prairie
by seashells and by a little vertigo
preceded by your sex
by what must be done with it,
by your blood held in white bunches
preceded by and livid from those one hundred dead inside your
    blood
preceded by departures sown into the wind that passes
and that folds them back into the shade
preceded by monkeys
preceded by hawthorn and beatitude
(neither the patience nor enough eyes
I look at you)
preceded by solstices turning against the equinox
and by paper hearts
preceded by great exhaustions into which the sea capsizes
that's two hundred dead and your
mouth
exhausted
and you are beautiful and
preceded by all those times when you are beautiful
pressed by the boat's bow
and so pressed to be

The Bubble Ball

Those are my abandoned cats, I feed them birds
those are my stiff birds, I dress them in flowers
that's life, fur and feather, in little whitened piles
Under the heavy blue I listen to the earth's lies
the sun will keep shining over a thousand charnel houses
blue eyes will keep becoming bluer for love
and the ghosts of some women will lie on top of me
each with her breasts each with her death
still more sheep will burst at sea
and bubbles too in the evening
still daytime will stay for one thousand and two nights
and for all of this time I will not see you
we'll build images again in those minds
and for all of this time you will have white eyes
there will be no wind

Those are my long turtles, they're swimming back out of the
    sludge
with their rumpled skirts
their sniper rifles their mad forevers
they swim up toward the rain, they are my great blind girls
my foxes of tears, they don't even have tongues left
On the corner of silence there is a green path
that waits for carcasses—
they will come, love follows
there are four round towers that watch the sky go by
ponds of molten lead, of bald sinking children
there are stone bubbles blowing stone bubbles
great naked stags on the highway
hollow suns, there is no wind
And for all of this time we see nothing
it is daytime

Those are the other and the pond, two stops in time
the shade is a great rabbit
and the pillow is swarming with orange rats
the other and the screen have turned over a new leaf
I cannot see your skin
the evenings are longer than evenings
death grows, cuts its prices
the great blue thing hangs in the cemetery, off blue pitchforks
it falls as fast as the night, it catches us unsuspecting
with all of this snow I can't see tomorrow
O, I so preferred the rain, the long swords of the rain
the little angels painted milkshake style
I want to scc you again with your too-big mouth

Written for the Occasion

Onto three ducks
grayer than the grass
the rain fell
the sea fell
Onto your very pink knees
the night fell too
the rain fell,
and onto the moose in its desert
tongues of salt and rancid butter
The curve of your hips saw the year off
the fire from the windowpanes rose into our cheeks
Then there came suns and knits older than that
winter skies inside mirrors
iced and bloodied mud,
there came long girls armed with gods
scattered dwarves and the tips of lances
ramps of snow hiding their iron
and there came small creatures
small lepers, small moons
there came maces and sluices
bronze rain on the paper
We wrote with our mouths open
the price of things we would forget
the sound of dogs when you break them
the nights of hunting in the hallways
we wrote for the occasion
for the tender grass of knives
an orange monkey in our hearts
we wrote the word coal
There came frictions, returns
low-warp combats
there came April children

with many purple eyes
who didn't write
and who touched the wind
Enormous flowers
guided the fire toward the curtains

Iris Waterfall

to Guy Cabanel

I was living at the foot of the waterfall
I was young and humid
Every thousand years I changed my shadow
I ate dormice and butterflies
But then nothing came

The stones rolled in the sunlight
There was sunlight once or twice a night
and elongated creatures that laughed like women
there were women once or twice a dream
I don't know what all of this is

In winter, caravans caravels
waited for us to make up words
before moving right past me
An orange foam covered the sky
I'd wake up late

Summer nights
I'd gamble on the evening primrose, on electric trout
on the impatience of red
I'd gamble on my skins in forests that were being born
Irises grew inside the devil's eye

The Bridge

to Robert Lagarde

A young mountain
Let's take her when she comes out of the water,
naked
in her fern boots
Let's take her before the sun does, before memory does,
before that first winter,
let's take her at the same time the wolves do
let's take her with red lips
There's a bridge
She doesn't see it, she doesn't see bridges,
she is from long before bridges
from before phantoms
Stones roll inside her eyes,
stones and clouds
and the head of the storm
Let's take her when it's still easy enough
and when her flank is warm,
barely conscious ourselves
of our atrocious perspiring
and of the weasels' laugh
Let's take the young mountain,
peek after peek, gorge until engorged
Before the bridge, before
the white ruins of love

The Ocean of the Washhouse and Even the Rust Is Blue

Thirty years later I saw your room
You couldn't dream it more plain
I never pictured you so bare
Four white walls a grey door
another door opening onto that countryside
where you opened more than your legs for me
All of my thoughts have their origin in those days
the grass's growth, hanging off the barns
and the words of your silence
All of love speaks through your mouth
all of love speaks in hazelnuts
in blackberries, whips, and muddy paths—
the gold of your sex burned the world away
All of love speaks in riddles
in dead cats in crossed fingers
all of love speaks through the embrace
of those two gazes on either side of the well
all of love speaks through your laughter
when we fell heart against hay
Wet horses, hair like May

We drank all of the rain
All of the spit all of the shade
All of love dies if the well sinks

The Lawn

It's a great lawn
its golf and its light
and it's a crow painted
on the eye of a lamprey
Now it's dawn inside its lantern
a languid string
a strong windmill grinding the sky,
it's a life made of plaster
on the great lawn
There's a sleeping stag
in his grand stag blood
and no one is holding the bow
There are other great things
like a woman with great breasts
holding her dogs of mist
the ocean on its pedestal
And it's such a great lawn
nothing forbids it from burning
nothing forbids it from screaming
nothing forbids it from making
silence fall upon her ashes
silence fall upon the rain
and now it's dawn
and she is shaking the bones
like too much jewelry
it's the great grey remains
of dawn on the patios
the chains, the forgotten memory of the chains
and that sharp little sound

Hurry

Stop it with your eagles
The eagles of your breasts
And your other birds of prey
The eagle owls of your buttocks
The bearded vulture of your cunt
The vulture of my liver
Stop it, Love, stop it
I didn't know you then
That day when I saw on the Loire River
Those long black wading birds
I was holding the light
On either side of me
Night was about to fall
I thought I was holding it together
I didn't know you then
I didn't feel the blood
Pushing its white wave forward
But then you threw
Your face at my face
Your eagles into my hands
Your eagle owl buttocks
You threw me, Lark,
Against your mirror
And those long wading birds
Those very long wading birds
Tonight it is snowing
And all the birds are blue
Small corpses, cutting their teeth
I love your teeth
I am holding my head
Inside your hands

The Night

The night is mad, gently so
The night gently kills the madmen
She ties their long hair to the ropes of fate
And pulls
She ties their naked horses together
And pushes hard
The night takes back the madmen and their white forced
    laughter at reason
Small eagles small drums
The night makes the small eagles mad too
A bald child is hatching a bald chicken
The night is mad with its elbows
Placed on the table of the day
With its wolves in a hurry to come back tomorrow
No one waits for love with their breasts in the clouds like that
No one waits for him to come
Run a red light run on empty
No one the lamp no one the temples on either side of the face
No one lingering so short of breath
The night runs herself through the cold alleys
She is pink and blind
The night drops flesh into the sharks' jaws
She serves us death, the night is mad
The night is a shark in a bed of irises
An excessive image that does not say quite enough
How the night is without you, how no one waits
For me to find the daylight again

A Walk With

to Nicole Espagnol

In the spring of that year, 1358, the peasants of northern France did not sow their fields any more.
                                    —*Hans Koning*

It wasn't the war every day,
sometimes you could follow the path
walk after a white cloud in the sky—
the red would come with evening
You could sometimes assemble words
Not for long:
in a shrubbery of skulls
a shield would sing
you'd constantly pass this riderless horse
naked like a woman and like the winter
the water ran yellow when it ran
sows were crucified, mermaids were burned
our teeth laughed
the first sound in the morning, it was of the bludgeon hitting
      flesh
Stumps spoke
stumps assembled words,
dew embers ocean,
there was but one kingdom for all of those horses,
there were capes, hedgehogs
gnomes riding dwarves
toads on lips
It wasn't the war every day,
since your breasts were there
your flamboyant threshold

since you were my she-fox
my path to you,
since you weren't nailed to the barns every day
Sometimes we'd lose pounds of ash,
we'd count the gallows, in the evening, to fall asleep
it wasn't like that every day
we'd carry baskets of heads, go plant them,
we really should feed ourselves
o my green fox in the night of the fountains
The stags would walk by far from the smoke
become tigers, become gods,
the stags were the only real men
the does shone deep inside the caverns
We took shoes off of the stones, we hung up our boots
on our bones we wore nothing but petticoats of fog
we slept in saddles, we saddled sleep
at the speed poets work
It was the war every day,
deaf rams and thick roses

The Useless

The useless regards us through its fixed eyes
The alcohol of the great dead burns at the stake of old age,
burns the ax of the butchers
We'll believe it's nice out, we'll believe the spark:
the useless regards us through its eyes of wax

Deader than a rat, more king than dead
is the useless
with its girls in the bushes
and its intersections outside the window—
the useless with its heavy arms,
with its expansive breath spreading on the screen

There are naked dusts and uncertain creatures,
those are not the useless
There are the roses of the useless
there is the swaying of the useless
mountains of mountains
and the jellyfish of time

The useless is our being there,
and being there is what we are not

Red Water

And then our world wiped away its blood
There was no other world but this world
we'd have to go on,
wash it all in red water

The young girls first
so again there might be
white necks, white teeth
so we could start gnawing again
at the death of tomorrow

Then, the animals
all of the animals in the red water
so again there might be fur,
lethargy, delight
gold in forest clearings
and great silent cries

Then, wash from their waters the red water
for the world to get its mirror back
for the world to watch itself go by

Then, wash from the fire the red ashes
of the bone set inside the smoke,
then wash the fire with open eyes
those totems of everything, then wash the sky

The worst is never ripe
The worst
is that final stage of memory
is the worst recurring once more,
the shrieking dust once more

We will have to wash the black water,
there is no other world but this world
This world,
the black iron of night.

I Don't

I don't dispute thistles with the wind
shadows with the winter
men with other men
I don't dispute fire with the burn
ash with the waking
I don't dispute water with the falls
But I do dispute flesh with the jaw
wine with assassins,
and love with its absence

I am a secondary route
they won't salt me in winter
So I stay with my creatures
furred ones, plastic ones
and gaze at the winter,
its raspberries and lagoons

I fly slowly
to the rescue of silence,
I don't fly at all
I tie the cold to its favors
springtime to its rope
I try on the night
What kills me does not make me stronger

The Wind in April 2007

to Stéphane Mirambeau

The wind that dries up those characters
that makes the countryside wild
livable and wild
and the scattered creatures
the wind that slices through the cap
the wind that pulls the sheets
and uncovers salamanders
the fire takes once more
the countryside is wildly livable
with its twisted blond hair
its twisted black hair
its twisted red hair
the wind opens the legs of the trees
it's always about love
and twisted horses
the wind
murmurs things to the boats
from one world into another
the wind rocks its butterflies
in one world they are white
and they are horses
and in the other they are black
and they are horses
the wind murmurs to the boats
it moves red rocks
brings to the roebuck the smell of the roebuck
and the terror of her own eyes back to the doe
the wind lifts that smell
one blackbird a year a kite in the dewdrop
a thousand wooden horses prancing in the boat

a thousand fleshy corpses
turning into wind which is turning into honey
one oppidum two oppida
the horse opined that the hedge had been crossed
In April 2007 the wind had black scissors

A Truth Told to the Loved Woman

The truth is never naked,
it wears a brambly dress
The wind at its back
incites no wings to flap,
its tongue is a small hook
its eyes luminous mass graves
Merely the shadow of a door
and the dust is off
to recreate the world

Do You...

Do you have red lips
Do you have red lips when you love me
Do you have black lips
Do you have lips
Do you know if death is a star
Do you know if you can see it in a mirror
Do you know if the weather is beautiful the day after you die
Do you know if it's as beautiful as your lips when you love me
Do you love me
Do I see myself in your mirror
Do you have a mirror
Why don't I have one
What are you doing with your lips
Do you know if they're red when the weather is beautiful the
    day after you die
Do you know if they're white when you don't love me
Do you not love me
Do you know if the earth loved us, do you remember
Do you know if the earth loved us when you had lips
When it turned white, do you remember
Why does my head hurt, do you remember
Why is there a snake on the earth's mirror
Do you know if that's just the way it is

Acknowledgments

Grateful acknowledgment is made to the journals where some of these translations first appeared:

Absinthe: New European Writing: "The Lovers" and "The Images"
Asymptote: "Glimmers" and "The Foam of Lions"
Cerise Press: "A Treatise on Wolves"
Circumference: "Furniture," "The Bridge," "The Night," and "Hurry"
FIELD: "September Alone"
Guernica: "Boulevard des Invalides"
Gulf Coast: "A Few of the Words I Was Mysteriously Allowed Until Now" and "It Will Come in My Left Lung"
Hayden's Ferry Review: "The Twisted Eye"
Mead: The Magazine of Literature and Libations: "Sunday" and "The Snow"
Tongue: "Iris Waterfall"
Washington Square: "Sunday" and "Written for the Occasion"

Many thanks to Sasha Fletcher for co-translating "September Alone." And thank you to Robert Stewart for his help with "The Lovers" and "The Images." Thank you too to Elizabeth Clark Wessel, Iris Cushing, Marina Blitshteyn, Jay Deshpande, Joshua Daniel Edwin, Sam Ross, Tanya Paperny, and Julia Guez for their support in the eleventh hour.

Much gratitude to Atelier de l'Agneau, Cadex Éditions, Pierre Bordas et Fils, L'Escampette Éditions, L'Oie de Cravan, and Seghers, who published Peuchmaurd's original texts and, through their generosity, allowed this project to be completed.

Many thanks to Martha Collins, David Young, David Walker, and Marco Seiryu Wilkinson for their outstanding support of this project.

And finally, many thanks to Antoine Peuchmaurd, Anne-Marie Beeckman, George-Henri Morin, Jean-Yves Bériou, Jean-Pierre Paraggio, and Laurent Albarracin for their invaluable insights.